cooking classics
korea

cooking classics

korea

A STEP-BY-STEP COOKBOOK

chun nam won

mc Marshall Cavendish
Cuisine

The publisher wishes to thank Pyrex Metalware, Visions and
Ekco 123 for the loan of kitchen utensils used in this book.

Editor : Sylvy Soh
Designer : Lynn Chin Nyuk Ling
Photographer : Joshua Tan, Elements By The Box

Copyright © 2010 Marshall Cavendish International (Asia) Private Limited

Published by Marshall Cavendish Cuisine
An imprint of Marshall Cavendish International
1 New Industrial Road, Singapore 536196

Other Marshall Cavendish Offices:
Marshall Cavendish International. PO Box 65829, London, EC1P 1NY, UK • Marshall Cavendish
Corporation, 99 White Plains Road, Tarrytown NY 10591-9001, USA • Marshall Cavendish International
(Thailand) Co Ltd. 253 Asoke, 12th Flr, Sukhumvit 21 Road, Klongtoey Nua, Wattana, Bangkok 10110,
Thailand • Marshall Cavendish (Malaysia) Sdn Bhd, Times Subang, Lot 46, Subang Hi-Tech Industrial
Park, Batu Tiga, 40000 Shah Alam, Selangor Darul Ehsan, Malaysia

Marshall Cavendish is a trademark of Times Publishing Limited

National Library Board, Singapore Cataloguing-in-Publication Data

Won, Chun Nam.
Korea : a step-by-step cookbook / Chun Nam Won. – Singapore : Marshall Cavendish Cuisine, c2010.
p. cm. – (Cooking classics)
Includes index.
ISBN-13 : 978-981-4302-53-1

1. Cookery, Korean. I. Title. II. Series: Cooking classics.

TX724.5.K65
641.59519 -- dc22   OCN630352970

Printed in Malaysia by Times Offset (M) Sdn Bhd

contents

introduction

Like many other food cultures in the world, Korean cuisine is deeply reflective of its fascinating culture, and stems from a rich, colourful history that is interlinked with influences from China. At the same time, Korean cuisine also reflects the bountiful produce of its land, in its use of fresh, seasonal ingredients.

Korean cuisine is wide and varied, from popular street snacks to unique dishes that are classified according to the various regions in both North and South Korea. The northern, central and southern regions feature a variety of dishes that are unique to their part of the land, with emphasis on the produce that region is famous for.

The Koreans' love and respect for food is seen in their relationship with food. Above mere enjoyment, the nutritional value of food is of utmost importance. Food is seen as medicine for the body, and something that can be used to heal, detoxify and nourish. Cooking techniques seldom feature a heavy use of fats to fry and flavour food; instead, minimal or little oil is used, and food is often grilled, stir-fried, simmered, steamed, braised or pickled. A typical Korean meal will always have a well-balanced variety of meat, vegetables and carbohydrates, most of which are lightly seasoned and cooked so as to allow their natural flavours to shine through.

Various dishes are usually eaten according to season, and in relation to health. In summer, the warming ginseng chicken soup (*samgyetang*) is heavily consumed as Koreans believe that the nutrients in the dish promote detoxification of the body while replenishing essential nutrients at the same time. Beef is also heavily consumed, and a favourite way of cooking it is through grilling, such as in the case for *bulgogi*. Kimchi, which is eaten all year round, is revered for being a rich source of vitamins and lactobacilli, a food-cultured bacteria that aids digestion. Soups are treated as a vital source of nourishment, and are consumed or promoted according to the health needs of a person. Desserts are seldom taken after meals, as there is seldom room left for it. However, one should not overlook the wonderful variety of *tteok* and *hangwa* (sweets and snacks made with glutinous rice).

Korean cuisine is now enjoyed by many different cultures all over the world. Within Asia, its demand is particularly elevated, perhaps due to the many Korean drama serials that consist of scenes involving food and eating.

Korean dishes are not difficult to recreate. The recipes and notes in this cookbook will help you to understand and appreciate Korean cuisine, and most importantly, to re-create authentic Korean dishes in your home kitchen.

cooking techniques

cooking heat

The good control of heat is essential for cooking Korean dishes well. A low, steady heat is suitable for cooking soups and stews so that the flavour of the ingredients can be drawn out and employed to their maximum potential, and delicate ingredients which have a tendency to disintegrate during the cooking process are kept intact. Medium to medium-high heat is typically employed for stir-fries where thin slices of meat or seafood are cooked quickly and with constant tossing motions in order to prevent juices from drying out and causing the food to be tough and overcooked. Extremely high heat is seldom used, although a pot of water brought to a rigorous boil over high heat helps to scald meats to remove scum before they are used in cooking. Ensure that cooking utensils such frying pans are always heated thoroughly before cooking to ensure an even distribution of heat.

salting

The use of salt in Korean cooking extends beyond adding flavour to dishes. Salting vegetables with a high water content helps to extract liquid so that the vegetables do not turn soggy during the cooking or pickling process. Salt is also an essential ingredient for preserving food such as in the case of kimchi.

grilling

In modern Korean homes, grilling is done through the use of a grill pan or oven for the sake of convenience. However, grilling meat and vegetables over a charcoal fire produces a sweet, smoky flavour that conventional pans and ovens cannot reproduce. Regardless of the medium, ensure that the cooking heat is well-distributed so that the food does not burn or blacken too readily without cooking on the inside.

marinating

Marinating is always employed for meats in Korean cooking. Marinades vary from liquids such as fruit juice, soy bean paste, soy sauce, chilli paste, sesame oil and anchovy sauce, to ingredients such as chillies, garlic, spring onions, chilli powder, salt and pepper. Particularly interesting is the use of fruit juice in marinating meat—the enzymes from the juice break down the protein content in the meat, thus making it tender. Spring onions also feature heavily in the marinating process as they lend a unique flavour to the final dish.

Korean cooking techniques typically consist of salting, pickling, marinating, stir-frying and grilling.

pickling

Pickling was a necessary technique employed for preserving food for the cold winter months in the past. Today, pickled vegetables such as kimchi are enjoyed as a side dish and appetiser during meals. Contrary to popular belief, the Korean method of pickling does not employ the use of vinegar. Instead, pickling ingredients such as salt, garlic, chilli, ginger, soy sauce, chilli powder, preserved prawns, and spring onions are used, and yield pickled vegetables that are full of flavour while retaining their crunch. The fermenting process of pickling produces a high quantity of lactobacilli, a bacteria which aids digestion.

stir-frying

Stir-frying is a quick, easy way of cooking food. A spatula is used to 'push' the food around in a pan or wok, usually in a continuous motion, until the food is cooked. Meat and vegetables are cut into bite-size pieces to ensure quick and even cooking. Unless otherwise stated, a small amount of oil is poured into the wok and heated to the desired temperature. Dry ingredients or seasonings, such as garlic, ginger or spices are added and stir-fried until fragrant, before the main ingredients are added to the pan or wok.

side dishes
and appetisers

seasoned spinach 18

seasoned potatoes 21

seasoned lotus root 22

simmered beef and eggs in soy sauce 25

beef roll salad 26

top shell salad 29

assorted beef, vegetable and pancake platter 30

spring onion pancake 33

mung bean pancakes 34

shiitake mushroom pancakes 37

kimchi pancakes 38

seasoned spinach shigeumchi namul

A popular *banchan* (side dish), this simple but nutritious appetiser can be prepared in a matter of minutes. **Serves 4**

Chinese spinach 150 g (5$^1/_3$ oz)

Salt $^1/_2$ tsp

Iced water 500 ml (16 fl oz / 2 cups)

Seasoning

Finely chopped garlic $^1/_2$ tsp

Salt $^1/_3$ tsp

Light soy sauce 1 tsp

Sesame oil $^1/_2$ Tbsp

White sesame seeds 1 Tbsp

1 Prepare spinach. Trim and discard roots, then separate stems from leaves. Set aside.

2 Bring a pot of water to the boil. When water starts to boil, add salt. Place spinach stems in and cook for 2 minutes. Add leaves and cook for 1 minute.

3 Remove spinach stems and leaves from pot. Place in a colander and rinse under running water, then transfer to a bowl of iced water and submerge completely.

4 Remove spinach from iced water and squeeze water out with your hands. Place in a mixing bowl, then add ingredients for seasoning. Toss well before serving.

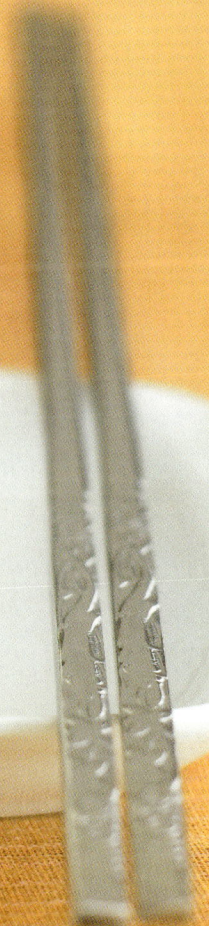

seasoned potatoes gamja jorim

Deliciously savoury and sweet, this simple potato dish can be eaten as a side dish or a light snack. **Serves 4**

Potatoes 350 g (12 oz)

Salt 1 tsp

Cooking oil 1 Tbsp

Light soy sauce 3 Tbsp

Water 125 ml (4 fl oz / ½ cup)

Mirin 2 Tbsp

Sugar 1 tsp

Glucose 2 Tbsp

Sesame oil 1 Tbsp

White sesame seeds 1 Tbsp

Sliced red chilli (optional)

1 Peel potatoes and slice into 2.5-cm (1-in) cubes. Bring about 500 ml (16 fl oz / 2 cups) water to the boil in a pot. Add potatoes and salt and cook for 3 minutes. Remove potatoes, drain and discard boiling water.

2 Heat oil in a frying pan over medium heat. Stir-fry potatoes for 2 minutes, then add soy sauce, water, mirin and sugar. Stir-fry potatoes so that they are evenly coated with sauce, and until the gravy has reduced to about two tablespoons.

3 Add glucose and mix well so that potatoes are evenly coated. Stir-fry for 5 minutes, then add sesame oil, sesame seeds and chilli if using. Toss well before removing from heat.

4 Dish out and serve immediately.

seasoned lotus root yun geun jorim

The delicately flavoured lotus root complements the seasoning ingredients in this side dish. **Serves 4**

Fresh lotus root 250 g (9 oz)

Cooking oil 2 Tbsp

Water 180 ml (6 fl oz / $^3/_4$ cup)

Sugar 2 Tbsp

Light soy sauce 2 Tbsp

Mirin 2 Tbsp

Dark soy sauce $^1/_2$ Tbsp

Glucose 2 Tbsp

Sesame oil 1 tsp

Sesame seeds 1 Tbsp

1 Peel lotus root and slice thinly. Heat oil in a frying pan over medium heat. Fry lotus root slices for about 3 minutes or until they turn slightly translucent.

2 Add water, sugar, light soy sauce and mirin to pan over medium heat, coating lotus root slices evenly. Stir-fry until there is only about 2 tablespoonfuls of gravy left in pan.

3 Add dark soy sauce and glucose and stir-fry for another 5 minutes. Increase heat to high and add sesame oil and seeds. Stir-fry for 1 more minute, coating lotus root slices evenly with sesame seeds.

4 Remove from heat and serve immediately.

simmered beef and eggs in soy sauce
jang jorim

This side dish features tenderly simmered melt-in-your-mouth beef in a deliciously savoury gravy. **Serves 4**

Eggs 2, at room temperature

Beef shin 600 g (1 lb 5^1/$_3$ oz)

Water 1.2 litres (40 fl oz / 5 cups)

Light soy sauce 180 ml (6 fl oz / ^{3}/$_4$ cup)

Sugar 4 tsp

Ginger 10 g (^{1}/$_3$ oz), peeled and sliced

Garlic 8 cloves

Red and green chillies 3–4, coarsely sliced

1 Place eggs in a pot and fill with water. Bring to the boil and cook eggs for 12–15 minutes. Remove eggs and place in a basin of cool water before peeling. Set eggs aside.

2 Slice beef shin into 5 x 5-cm (2 x 2-in) pieces. Set aside.

3 Fill a clean pot with 1.2 litres (40 fl oz / 5 cups) water and bring to the boil. Place beef in, reduce heat to low and leave to simmer for about 40 minutes. Test beef for doneness by piercing it with a chopstick. The beef is cooked if juices run clear. Remove beef and set aside. Leave stock to simmer until reduced to half the amount.

4 Mix light soy sauce and sugar in a bowl. Add some hot stock to dissolve sugar, then return mixture to pot. Add ginger, garlic and chillies to pot and bring to a gentle boil over low heat for 10 minutes or until stock has reduced to a thick gravy. Remove ginger slices and discard. Add eggs and leave to cook for another 5 minutes.

5 Remove pot from heat and slice eggs into halves. Dish contents of pot out into serving portions and serve immediately.

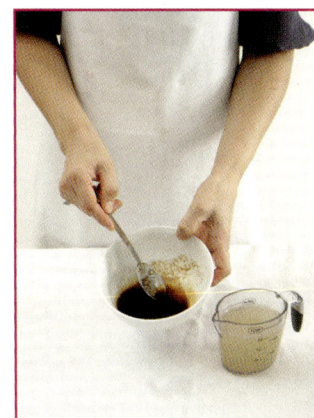

beef roll salad gogi pyun chae

These tender beef rolls are not only tasty but pretty to look at, making them great for serving at parties. **Serves 4**

Radish sprouts 100 g (3 ½ oz)

White onion 1, peeled

Cucumber 1

Beef tenderloin 300 g (11 oz)

Glutinous (sticky) rice flour 70 g
(2½ oz / ½ cup)

Vegetable oil as needed

Seasoning

Light soy sauce 2 Tbsp

Chinese cooking wine (Shaoxing) 1 Tbsp

Sesame oil 1 tsp

Sugar ½ Tbsp

Pear juice 1 Tbsp or grate ½ Korean pear
and squeeze to extract 1 Tbsp juice

Dipping sauce

Light soy sauce 1 Tbsp

Pear juice 1 Tbsp or grate ½ Korean pear
and squeeze to extract 1 Tbsp juice

Rice vinegar 1 Tbsp

Sugar ½ Tbsp

Prepared mustard 1 Tbsp

1   Trim roots from sprouts, then slice sprouts into 5-cm (2-in) lengths from root end. Slice onion and cucumber into thin, 5-cm (2-in) slices. Slice beef thinly. Set aside.

2   Combine seasoning ingredients in a mixing bowl. Place beef slices and mix well. Leave to marinate for 20–30 minutes. Drain beef slices through a sieve, then coat evenly with flour.

3   Heat oil in a frying pan over medium heat. Fry beef slices for 3–5 minutes or until they reach medium-well doneness.

4   Combine ingredients for dipping sauce. Transfer to a sauce dish. Divide vegetables into equal portions as per beef slices. Roll each slice up with vegetables.

5   Serve beef rolls immediately, with dipping sauce on the side.

top shell salad gol baeng e mu chim

The piquant, spicy flavour of this salad makes it a perfect way to start a meal. **Serves 4**

Top shell 1 can, about 150 g (5⅓ oz)

Japanese cucumber ½

Red chilli 1

Green chilli 1

Spring onions (scallions) 100 g (3½ oz)

Salad dressing

Corn syrup 1 Tbsp

Chilli powder 1 Tbsp

Korean chilli paste 1 Tbsp

Light soy sauce 1 Tbsp

Minced garlic 2 tsp

Salt a pinch

White rice vinegar 2 Tbsp

Sugar 1 tsp

Sesame oil 1 tsp

White sesame seeds a pinch

1 Drain top shell from can, discarding juices. Bring a small pot of water to the boil and blanch top shell briefly. Remove from heat and rinse well with cold water. Slice each piece in half. Set aside.

2 Slice cucumber into half lengthwise, then cut further into thin semi-circles. Slice chillies into half lengthwise and remove seeds. Slice into thin, even strips. Trim off and discard root end of spring onions and slice into 5-cm (2-in) lengths.

3 Prepare salad dressing. Combine all ingredients well in a mixing bowl. Add top shell, spring onion, chilli and cucumber slices to dressing. Toss ingredients well to season thoroughly.

4 Serve salad chilled, garnished with sesame seeds.

  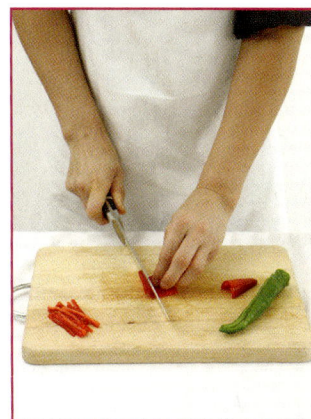

assorted beef, vegetable and pancake platter
gu jeol pan

Traditionally, this dish was served only to Korean royalty. Today, this assorted platter is enjoyed by everyone regardless of their social status. **Serves 4**

Young cucumber 1

Salt as needed

Dried wood ear fungus 15 g (^{1}/$_2$ oz)

Carrot 125 g (4^1/$_2$ oz)

Fresh bamboo shoots 150 g (5^1/$_3$ oz)

Beef 150 g (5^1/$_3$ oz), thinly sliced

Fresh shiitake mushrooms 6, thinly sliced

Cooking oil as needed

Eggs 3, yolks and whites separated and beaten lightly

Marinade (combined)

Light soy sauce 1 Tbsp

Ground black pepper a pinch

Sugar 1 tsp

Minced garlic 1 tsp

Pancakes

Plain (all-purpose) flour 70 g (2^1/$_2$ oz / ^{1}/$_2$ cup)

Salt ^{1}/$_4$ tsp

Water 150 ml (5^1/$_3$ fl oz)

Dipping sauce (combined)

Korean mustard or any preferred mustard 2 Tbsp,

Brown rice vinegar 2 Tbsp

Sugar ^{1}/$_2$ Tbsp

Water 1 Tbsp

Salt ^{1}/$_2$ tsp

1   Cut cucumber into 4-cm (1^1/$_2$-in) strips. Place in a bowl and sprinkle with salt. Leave for 10 minutes or until cucumber start to exude liquid. Squeeze strips to remove excess liquid. Set aside. Soak fungus in water for 30 minutes or until softened. Drain, then slice into thin 4-cm (1^1/$_2$-in) strips. Slice carrot and bamboo shoots likewise.

2   Place beef and mushrooms in separate bowls, then divide marinade between bowls and mix well. Heat a little oil in a frying pan over medium heat. Fry beef until cooked. Remove from heat and set aside. Reheat pan and fry mushrooms for 3–5 minutes. Remove from heat and set aside.

3   Heat a little oil in a clean frying pan over medium heat. In separate batches, stir-fry cucumber, fungus, carrot and bamboo shoots with a pinch of salt for 2–3 minutes or until tender but still firm. Remove from heat and set aside.

4   Prepare egg yolk and egg white omelettes (see page 54).

5   Prepare pancakes. Place flour and salt in a mixing bowl. Add water gradually while mixing until a batter is formed. Strain batter through a fine mesh sieve to remove any lumps. Heat a little oil in a clean frying pan over low-medium heat. Spoon about 1 Tbsp batter into pan and fry until bubbles appear on surface of pancake. Remove pancake from heat. Repeat step until batter is used up.

6   To serve, stack pancakes neatly in the middle of a round serving plate. Arrange cooked ingredients around pancakes. Serve immediately with dipping sauce on the side.

spring onion pancake hamul pa jeon

Chewy, with a lightly crisp crust, this tasty pancake is flavoured with spring onions, a favoured vegetable in Korean cuisine. **Serves 4**

Squid 100 g (3¹/₂ oz)

Prawns 100 g (3¹/₂ oz)

Spring onions (scallions) 200 g (7 oz)

Chives 50 g (1²/₃ oz)

Glutinous (sticky) rice flour 50 g (1²/₃ oz)

Plain (all-purpose) flour 150 g (5¹/₃ oz)

Water 400 ml (13¹/₃ fl oz / 1²/₃ cups)

Eggs 2, beaten

Cooking oil as needed

Red chilli 1, seeded and thinly sliced

Dipping sauce (combined)

Light soy sauce 4 Tbsp

Chilli powder 1 Tbsp

White rice vinegar 2 Tbsp

Finely chopped spring onion (scallion) 1 Tbsp

Minced garlic ¹/₂ Tbsp

White sesame seeds 2 Tbsp

Sesame oil 2 tsp

Sugar 1 tsp

1 Separate squid head from body. Rinse and set aside. Clean squid tube by removing innards and pulling away as much of the skin as possible. Rinse well. Chop coarsely. Peel prawns and chop coarsely.

2 Lay spring onions flat on a chopping board. Use the flat side of a knife blade to bruise and flatten root ends by pressing down firmly. Cut spring onions and chives into 12-cm (5-in) lengths. Set aside.

3 Combine flours in a mixing bowl. Gradually add water and one beaten egg, mixing thoroughly until a smooth batter is formed. Add half portion of squid and prawns to batter.

4 Add remaining portion of squid and prawns to the other beaten egg.

5 Heat a little oil in a frying pan over medium heat. Pour in batter and swirl it so it spreads out evenly. Arrange spring onions, chives and chilli in an even layer over batter.

6 When pancake is about to set, spoon egg mixture over spring onions, chives and chilli, spreading it evenly. Reduce heat to low and carefully flip pancake over to cook on the other side. Pancake should be light golden brown on both sides.

7 Serve pancake immediately with dipping sauce on the side.

mung bean pancakes bindaedduk

These easy-to-make pancakes yield a creamy, satisfying mouthful, and are popular with children. **Serves 4**

Bean sprouts 250 g (9 oz)

Mung beans 250 g (9 oz), washed and soaked in water for 3 hours

Water 500 ml (16 fl oz / 2 cups)

Onion 1, peeled and sliced

Glutinous (sticky) rice flour 80 g (3 oz)

Pork 200 g (7 oz), finely sliced

Cabbage kimchi (see page 42) 200 g (7 oz)

Spring onions (scallions) 50 g (1²/₃ oz)

Red chilli (optional) 1, seeded and sliced

Salt a pinch

Dipping sauce (see page 33) 1 quantity

Marinade

Finely chopped spring onion (scallion) 1 Tbsp

Grated ginger 1 Tbsp

Salt 1 Tbsp

Sesame oil 1 Tbsp

Sesame seeds a pinch

Ground black pepper a pinch

1 Pick tails off bean sprouts, then rinse and drain well. Set aside.

2 Drain mung beans and place in a blender together with water and onion slices. Blend until fine. Add flour to blended mixture and mix well until a thick batter is formed.

3 Bring a pot of water to the boil. Blanch bean sprouts for 1–2 minutes, then remove and drain. Leave to cool slightly, then squeeze bean sprouts to remove excess water. Set aside.

4 Combine ingredients for marinade in a mixing bowl. Add pork and mix well, then add kimchi, bean sprouts, spring onions, chilli and salt. Add batter and mix well.

5 Heat a little oil in a frying pan over medium heat. When pan is hot, spoon in 2–3 Tbsp batter to make palm-size pancakes. Cook 3–4 pancakes each time, depending on the size of your pan. Fry pancakes on both sides until golden brown.

6 Garnish pancakes as desired and serve immediately with dipping sauce on the side.

shiitake mushroom pancakes pyogo jeon

Although not a pancake dish in the strictest sense, the stuffed mushrooms caps resemble mini pancakes and make a terrific party finger food. **Serves 4**

Fresh shiitake mushrooms 15

Minced beef 150 g (5¹/₃ oz)

Firm bean curd 100 g (3¹/₂ oz)

Plain (all-purpose) flour 70 g
(2¹/₂ oz / ¹/₂ cup)

Egg 1

Cooking oil

Dipping sauce (see page 33) 1 quantity

Marinade (combined)

Light soy sauce 1 Tbsp

Sugar ¹/₂ Tbsp

Finely chopped spring onion (scallion)
¹/₂ Tbsp

Finely minced garlic 1 Tbsp

White sesame seeds 1 Tbsp

Ground black pepper a pinch

Sesame oil 2 tsp

1 Prepare mushrooms. Bring a pot of lightly salted water to the boil. Add mushrooms to boiling water and cook for 1–2 minutes, then drain and pat dry with paper towels. Set aside.

2 Place beef in a bowl and pour marinade over. Mix well, then refrigerate and leave until needed.

3 Wrap bean curd with a piece of muslin cloth and squeeze out as much water as possible. Transfer drained bean curd to a bowl and mash with a spoon. Add marinated beef and mix well.

4 Coat the undersides of a mushroom cap with flour, then stuff with bean curd and beef mixture. Repeat for remaining mushrooms.

5 Lightly grease a frying pan with oil and heat over medium heat. Dab some flour over stuffing and coat with egg. When pan is hot, add 4–5 mushrooms, placing them filling-side down on pan. Cook for 3–5 minutes, then flip over and cook other side for 1–2 minutes. Repeat to cook remaining mushrooms.

6 Serve immediately with dipping sauce on the side.

kimchi pancakes kimchi jeon

These lightly spicy pancakes can be easily whipped up for a quick snack. **Serves 4**

Squid 1

Prawns 50 g (1²/₃ oz)

Cabbage kimchi (see page 42) 250 g (9 oz)

Chives 25 g (³/₄ oz)

Spring onion (scallion) 25 g (³/₄ oz)

Plain (all-purpose) flour 1 cup

Potato flour 4 Tbsp

Water 250 ml (8 fl oz / 1 cup)

Cucumber (optional) ¹/₂, cut into strips
   using a vegetable peeler

Cooking oil as needed

1 Separate squid head from body. Rinse and set aside. Clean squid tube by removing innards and pulling away as much of the skin as possible. Rinse well. Cut into 1-cm (¹/₂-in) pieces. Peel prawns and cut likewise.

2 Slice kimchi, chives and spring onion into 1-cm (¹/₂-in) lengths. Set aside.

3 In a mixing bowl, combine both types of flour. Gradually add water and mix into a smooth batter. Add chopped ingredients and mix well.

4 Lightly grease a frying pan with oil and heat over medium heat. When pan is hot, ladle about 2–3 Tbsp batter into pan to make palm-size pancakes. Cook in batches of 3–4, depending on the size of your pan. Fry pancakes on both sides until golden brown.

5 Garnish with cucumber strips if desired and serve immediately.

kimchi

cabbage kimchi 42

cucumber kimchi 45

radish kimchi 46

watery kimchi 49

white kimchi 50

cabbage kimchi kimchi

Cabbage kimchi is the most popular and definitive kimchi dish in Korean cuisine, and it is practically a staple in Korean homes. **Serves 4**

Chinese (napa) cabbage 2 heads

Coarse salt 250 g (9 oz / 1 cup)

Red chillies 6

Onion 1, peeled and finely minced

Korean preserved prawns (shrimps) 60 g (2$^1/_3$ oz)

Anchovy sauce 3 Tbsp

Finely minced garlic 3 Tbsp

Grated ginger 2 Tbsp

Korean chilli powder 120 g (4$^1/_2$ oz / 1 cup)

White radish 1, cut into 4-cm (1$^1/_2$-in) strips

Spring onions (scallions) 50 g (1$^2/_3$ oz), cut into 4-cm (1$^1/_2$-in) lengths

Sugar 1–2 Tbsp

Salted water

Salt 125 g (4$^1/_2$ oz / $^1/_2$ cup)

Water 1 litre (32 fl oz / 4 cups)

1 Make salted water by combining salt and water in a large mixing bowl. Mix well and set aside.

2 Make a cut halfway down cabbage lengthwise, then split the rest of the cabbage apart using your hands. Repeat for other cabbage head. Immerse cabbage in salted water briefly, then remove, drain and sprinkle liberally with coarse salt. Leave aside for 3–4 hours.

3 Make a slit down the length of each chilli. Remove the white pith and seeds. Leave chillies to soak in a bowl of water for 30 minutes. After chillies have been soaked, remove, drain and mince until fine. Combine with minced onion and set aside.

4 Combine preserved prawns, anchovy sauce, minced garlic, grated ginger and chilli powder in a mixing bowl and mix well. Add minced chilli and onion mixture, radish, spring onions and sugar and mix well.

5 Pack pickling mixture evenly between the leaves of both cabbage heads. Roll cabbage leaves up tightly from the base towards the frilly part of the leaves to ensure that pickling mixture is held tightly between the leaves.

6 Pack cabbages into airtight containers, seal and refrigerate for 1–2 days before consuming. Cabbage kimchi can be stored for up to 2 weeks refrigerated. If a stronger sour-tasting kimchi is desired, leave at room temperature for a day before refrigerating.

Note: Wear disposable gloves when handling chillies as the capsaicin in the chillies may leave a burning sensation on your skin.

cucumber kimchi ooi kimchi

This crunchy and spicy, chilled cucumber kimchi is particularly refreshing on a hot day. **Serves 4**

Japanese cucumbers 10

Salt 4 Tbsp

Chinese chives 200 g (7 oz)

Carrots 85 g (3 oz)

Korean chilli powder 6 Tbsp

Sugar 1 Tbsp

Korean preserved prawns (shrimps)
2 Tbsp, finely minced

Finely minced garlic 2 Tbsp

Finely chopped spring onion (scallion)
2 Tbsp

White sesame seeds a pinch

1 Scrub cucumbers with salt, then rinse with water.

2 Trim the ends of each cucumber, then cut into 5-cm (2-in) lengths. Place cucumbers on a cut side so it stands upright, then cut down the length of each cucumber horizontally and vertically (like a cross) without cutting through completely.

3 Cut chives and carrots into 1-cm ($^1/_2$-in) strips. Place in a mixing bowl, then add remaining ingredients and mix well.

4 Wrap cucumbers in a clean tea towel and gently squeeze them of excess water. Stuff cucumbers with chive and carrot mixture.

5 Pack cucumbers into airtight containers, seal and refrigerate for at least a day before consuming. Cucumber kimchi can be stored for up to 1 week refrigerated.

radish kimchi ggak ddu gi

As a vegetable with neutral flavours, white radish holds the various seasoning ingredients for this kimchi well. **Serves 4**

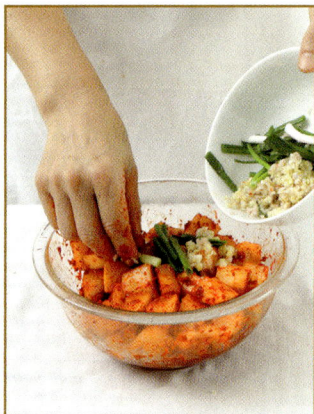

White radishes 2

Sugar 2 Tbsp

Salt 1$^1/_2$ Tbsp + more for seasoning (optional)

Garlic 8 cloves, peeled

Korean preserved prawns (shrimps) 3 Tbsp

Finely minced ginger 1 tsp

Korean chilli powder 60 g (2 oz), or slightly less if a less spicy kimchi is preferred

Spring onions (scallions) 3, cut into 3-cm (1$^1/_4$-in) lengths

1 Peel radishes, then cut into 1.5-cm ($^3/_4$-in) thick rounds and then into cubes. Place radish in a bowl and add sugar and salt. Set aside for 30 minutes. Drain off any excess water from radish but do not rinse radish. Set aside.

2 Combine garlic, preserved prawns and ginger on a chopping board and mince until fine. Place in a mixing bowl.

3 Add radish, chilli powder, spring onions to mixing bowl. Mix well, adding a little salt to season, if desired.

4 Pack radish into airtight containers, seal and refrigerate and for 1–2 days before consuming. Radish kimchi can be stored for up to 1 week refrigerated.

watery kimchi na bak kimchi

This kimchi has a refreshing zing from the chilli powder and pear juice used in the recipe. **Serves 4**

Chinese (napa) cabbage 500 g
(1 lb 1½ oz)

White radish 1, small, peeled

Cucumber 1, scrubbed with salt, rinsed
and drained

Salt 3 Tbsp

Garlic 4 cloves, peeled

Red chillies 2, seeded and cut into 2.5-cm
(1-in) pieces

Spring onions (scallions) 50 g (1²/₃ oz),
cut into 5-cm (2-in) lengths

Kimchi base liquid

Korean chilli powder 2 Tbsp

Water 2.5 litres (80 fl oz / 10 cups)

Salt 3 Tbsp

Sugar ½ Tbsp

Grated ginger 1 Tbsp

Pear juice 125 ml (4 fl oz / ½ cup)
or grate 1–2 Korean pears and
squeeze to extract 125 ml
(4 fl oz / ½ cup) juice

1   Combine chilli powder and 500 ml (16 fl oz / 2 cups) water for kimchi base liquid in a bowl. Set aside while preparing other ingredients.

2   Peel and discard outer leaves of cabbage, leaving only the inner yellowish-white leaves. Cut leaves into 2.5-cm (1-in) pieces. Cut radish and cucumber likewise. Slice garlic thinly.

3   Place cabbage, radish and cucumber in a mixing bowl. Sprinkle salt over evenly, then set aside for 15–20 minutes. Rinse and drain well.

4   Place a sieve over a large bowl. Line sieve with a sheet of muslin cloth and pour chilli powder water into sieve. Squeeze muslin to extract chilli essence. Add remaining ingredients for kimchi base liquid to chilli essence and stir well.

5   Pack cabbage, radish, cucumber, chillies, spring onion and garlic into airtight containers and pour kimchi base liquid over. Seal and refrigerate overnight before serving. Watery kimchi can be stored for up to 1 week refrigerated, and should be served with the kimchi base liquid.

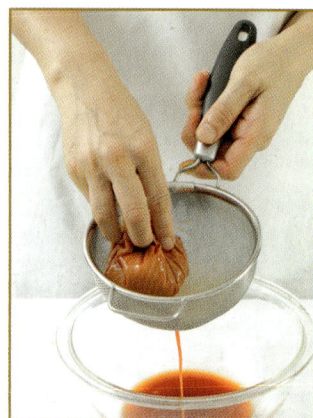

white kimchi baik kimchi

As it is not spicy, this kimchi is popular with Korean children. The chopped chestnuts and red dates add bite to this dish. **Serves 4**

Chinese (napa) cabbage 2 heads

Salt 375 g (13 oz / 1$^{1}/_{2}$ cups)

Water 1 litre (32 fl oz / 4 cups)

Chestnuts 5

Dried red dates 5

Korean pear 1

Garlic 8 cloves, peeled

Ginger 30 g (1 oz), peeled

Spring onions (scallions) 50 g (1$^{2}/_{3}$ oz)

White radish 1, peeled and thinly sliced

Pine nuts 1 Tbsp

Red chillies 4, seeded and finely sliced into strips

Anchovy sauce 2 Tbsp

Kimchi base liquid

Water 1.25 litres (40 fl oz / 5 cups)

Salt 2 Tbsp

Korean pear 1, grated and squeezed to extract juice

1   Make kimchi base liquid by combining water, salt and pear juice together in a mixing bowl. Set aside.

2   Halve cabbages (see page 42). Mix 125 g (4$^{1}/_{2}$ oz / $^{1}/_{2}$ cup) salt and water in a large bowl. Immerse cabbage in salted water briefly, then remove, drain and sprinkle liberally with remaining salt. Place in a bowl and leave aside for 2–3 hours before rinsing with fresh water.

3   Cut chestnuts and dates into thin strips. Peel, halve and core pear, then slice into 0.3-cm ($^{1}/_{10}$-in) thin slices. Slice garlic, ginger and spring onions into thin strips, then chop spring onions finely. Combine ingredients in a mixing bowl and add radish, pine nuts and chillies. Sprinkle anchovy sauce over and mix well.

4   Pack chestnut, pine nut and date mixture evenly between the leaves of both cabbage heads. Roll cabbage leaves up tightly from the base towards the frilly part of the leaves to ensure that the mixture is held tightly between the leaves.

5   Pack cabbages into airtight containers and pour kimchi base liquid over. Seal and keep at room temperature for 1 day, then refrigerate for 1–2 days before consuming. White kimchi can be stored for up to 1 week refrigerated, and should be served with the kimchi base liquid.

rice and noodles

stir-fried vermicelli 54

cold spicy kimchi noodles 57

beef soup noodles 58

kimchi dumplings 61

stir-fried spicy rice cakes 62

sliced rice cakes in soup 65

beef and vegetable hot stone rice 66

raw fish and vegetables with rice 69

stir-fried vermicelli jap chae

This popular Korean dish can be served as a main course or as a side dish. **Serves 4**

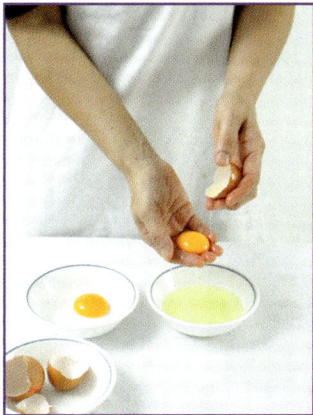

Dried sweet potato vermicelli 200 g (7 oz)

Chinese spinach 3–4 bunches, stems separated from leaves

Beef sirloin 150 g (5$\frac{1}{3}$ oz), sliced into strips

Fresh shiitake mushrooms 5, thinly sliced

Dried wood ear fungus 5 pieces, soaked in water until soft, then drained

Eggs 2

Vegetable oil 1 Tbsp

Sesame oil 2 Tbsp

Light soy sauce 4 Tbsp

Sugar 2 Tbsp

Carrot $\frac{1}{2}$, peeled and sliced into strips

Onion 1, peeled and thinly sliced

Salt a pinch

White sesame seeds 1 Tbsp

Marinade (combined)

Light soy sauce 1 Tbsp

Minced garlic 1 tsp

Sugar $\frac{1}{2}$ tsp

White sesame seeds 1 tsp

Sesame oil 1 tsp

Ground black pepper a pinch

1   Bring a pot of water to the boil. Blanch vermicelli briefly until softened, then remove, rinse under running water and drain. Using a pair of scissors, cut noodles into short lengths, approximately 5–8 cm (2–3 in).

2   Bring a fresh pot of water to the boil and cook spinach (see page 18). After removing spinach from water, drain in a colander and squeeze to remove excess water. Set aside.

3   Combine ingredients for marinade in a bowl. Add beef and mushrooms. Set aside to marinate until needed.

4   Coarsely tear softened wood ear fungus into smaller pieces. Set aside.

5   Crack eggs and separate yolks from whites. An easy way to do this is to crack an egg into a bowl and use your fingers to scoop the yolk out gently. Place yolk into another bowl. Cut egg whites (see page 58). Lightly beat egg yolks and whites separately. Heat a little oil in a frying pan over medium heat. Fry yolks into a thin omelette, then slice into thin strips. Repeat using egg whites.

6   Heat a frying pan over medium heat. Combine cut vermicelli with 1 Tbsp vegetable oil, 1 Tbsp sesame oil, 3 Tbsp soy sauce and 1 Tbsp sugar. Stir-fry for 1–2 minutes, tossing ingredients to mix well. Transfer to a mixing bowl and set aside.

7   Reheat frying pan over medium heat. Stir-fry carrot and onion and season with a pinch of salt. Remove from heat and set aside. Reheat frying pan or wok and stir-fry beef and mushrooms until beef is cooked.

8   Add spinach, omelette strips, wood ear fungus, vermicelli, sesame seeds, remaining sesame oil, soy sauce and sugar to pan. Toss well to mix and serve immediately.

cold spicy kimchi noodles bibim guksu

This noodle dish is commonly eaten during summer time in Korea. The sharp, spicy flavours rejuvenate a sluggish appetite, and the cold noodles provide relief from the heat. **Serves 4**

Beef 100 g (3^1/$_2$ oz), thinly sliced

Dried somen noodles 400 g (14^1/$_3$ oz)

Light soy sauce 2 Tbsp

Sugar 1 Tbsp

Sesame oil 2 Tbsp

Cooking oil as needed

Japanese cucumbers 2, thinly sliced, soaked in salted water for 10 minutes, then squeezed to remove excess water

Red chilli 1, seeded and sliced into strips

Kimchi

Cabbage kimchi (see page 42) 200 g (7 oz)

Sugar 1 tsp

Sesame oil 1 Tbsp

Sesame seeds 2 Tbsp

Beef marinade (combined)

Light soy sauce 1 tsp

Sugar ^{1}/$_2$ tsp

Minced garlic ^{1}/$_2$ tsp

Sesame oil 1 tsp

1 Prepare kimchi. Slice cabbage kimchi into 1-cm (^{1}/$_2$-in) pieces. Place in a bowl and add sugar, sesame oil and sesame seeds. Mix well and set aside.

2 Place beef slices in a bowl. Pour marinade over and leave to marinate until needed.

3 Bring a pot of water to the boil. Blanch somen noodles for 3–5 minutes or until slightly under al dente. Remove noodles and dunk them in a bowl of cold water to arrest the cooking process. Drain in a sieve and transfer to a bowl. Marinate noodles with soy sauce, sugar and sesame oil. Set aside.

4 Heat a frying pan over medium heat. Add a little oil and stir-fry cucumber strips lightly for 1–2 minutes or until just tender. Remove and set aside.

5 Reheat pan over medium heat and add a little oil. Stir-fry beef slices until cooked.

6 Divide noodles among 4 serving bowls. Top with beef and cucumber slices, kimchi and chilli strips. If desired, pour some kimchi pickling liquid over noodles. Serve immediately.

beef soup noodles jangteo guksu

Heartily flavoured, yet light on the palate, this noodle dish makes for a satisfying meal. **Serves 4**

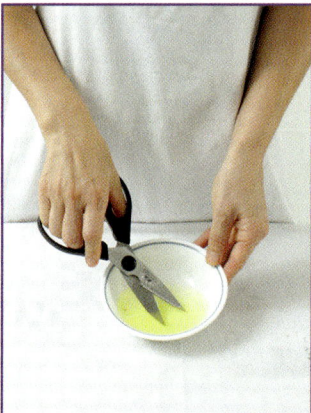

Beef brisket 300 g (11 oz)

Water 2 litres (64 fl oz / 8 cups)

Courgette (zucchini) $1/2$

Salt 1–2 pinches

Eggs 2

Dried somen noodles 300 g (11 oz)

Cooking oil as needed

Dried shiitake mushrooms 4, soaked in water to soften

Red chilli 1, seeded and sliced into strips

Beef marinade (combined)

Light soy sauce 1 Tbsp

Finely chopped spring onion (scallion) 1 Tbsp

Minced garlic 1 tsp

Sesame oil 1 tsp

Ground black pepper a pinch

Dipping sauce (combined)

Light soy sauce 2 Tbsp

Finely chopped spring onion (scallion) 1 tsp

Minced garlic $1/2$ tsp

Sesame oil 1 tsp

White sesame seeds 1 Tbsp

1 Cut beef brisket into 5-cm (2-in) pieces. In a pot, bring water to the boil. Add beef pieces and increase to high heat. Skim off scum and impurities that rise to the surface, then reduce heat to low. Leave beef to cook for about 1 hour or until tender. Remove beef pieces from heat and transfer to a bowl. Pour marinade over cooked beef and mix well. Leave aside until needed. Keep beef stock aside.

2 Cut courgette into thin strips. Place in a bowl and sprinkle salt over evenly. Leave to sit for about 10 minutes or until courgette strips start to exude liquid. Squeeze strips to remove excess liquid. Set aside.

3 Separate egg yolks and whites (see page 54). Using a pair of scissors, 'cut' egg whites to break up the albumen and to incorporate air into them. Lightly beat egg yolks and whites separately. Heat a little oil in a frying pan over medium heat. Fry egg yolks into a thin omelette, then slice into thin strips. Repeat with egg whites.

4 Cook somen noodles (see page 57). Divide noodles among 4 serving bowls and set aside.

5 Heat a frying pan over medium heat. Add a little oil and stir-fry courgette strips for 1–2 minutes. Remove and set aside. Keeping pan heated, add a little more oil and stir-fry beef and mushrooms until beef is cooked. Set aside.

6 To serve, reheat beef stock, adding salt to taste. Top noodles with omelette strips, sliced chilli, courgette, beef and mushrooms. Ladle hot stock into bowls and serve immediately, with dipping sauce on the side.

kimchi dumplings mandu

These dumplings are extremely versatile as they can be served steamed, boiled or fried. Make, then freeze these dumplings to enjoy them any time you want. **Serves 4**

Anchovy stock (see page 113) 1 quantity

Finely chopped spring onion (scallion) 1 Tbsp

Dumpling skin

Plain (all-purpose) flour 210 g (7 oz / $1^1/_2$ cups)

Salt $^1/_4$ tsp

Water 125 ml (4 fl oz / $^1/_2$ cup)

Filling

Minced pork or beef 150 g ($5^1/_3$ oz)

Bean sprouts 150 g ($5^1/_3$ oz)

Cabbage kimchi (see page 42) 150 g ($5^1/_3$ oz), finely chopped

Firm bean curd 125 g ($4^1/_2$ oz), rinsed and drained

Finely chopped spring onion (scallion) 2 Tbsp

Sesame oil 2 Tbsp

Salt 1 tsp

Ground black pepper to taste

Marinade (combined)

Light soy sauce 1 Tbsp

Sugar $^1/_2$ Tbsp

Finely chopped spring onion (scallion) 2 tsp

Minced garlic 1 tsp

Ground black pepper $^1/_4$ tsp

Dipping sauce (combined)

Light soy sauce 2 Tbsp

Water 1 Tbsp

Vinegar 2 Tbsp

Sugar 2 tsp

Chilli powder $^1/_2$ tsp

1 Prepare dumpling skin. Place flour and salt in a mixing bowl. Gradually add water and knead into a smooth dough. Wrap dough in a damp tea towel and leave aside for 30 minutes. Knead dough again and roll into a cylinder. Cut into 2.5-cm (1-in) portions. Roll each piece out on a lightly floured work surface into a thin sheet and set aside.

2 Place minced meat into a bowl with marinade. Set aside until needed.

3 Bring a pot of water to the boil and blanch bean sprouts for 1–2 minutes. Leave to cool slightly, then squeeze out excess water. Set aside.

4 Squeeze out any excess water from cabbage kimchi and bean curd.

5 Combine minced meat, bean sprouts, kimchi, bean curd, spring onion, sesame oil, salt and black pepper in a mixing bowl and mix well.

6 Spoon about 1 Tbsp filling onto a dumpling skin. Fold into a semi-circle, then bring the two 'corners' together and press to form an ingot-shaped dumpling. Repeat with remaining ingredients.

7 Bring anchovy stock to the boil over medium-high heat. Add dumplings to cook in batches. Dumplings are done when they float to the surface.

8 Spoon dumplings into serving bowls and ladle stock over. Serve immediately with dipping sauce on the side. Garnish with spring onion.

stir-fried spicy rice cakes tteokbokki

The chewy texture of the rice cakes are complemented by the spicy chilli paste seasoning, making each bite a delicious mouthful. **Serves 4**

Korean fish cake 40 g (1$^1/_3$ oz)

Chinese (napa) cabbage 30 g (1 oz)

Vegetable oil 1 Tbsp

Leek $^1/_2$, sliced into 5-cm (2-in) lengths

Anchovy stock (see page 113) 125 ml
(4 fl oz / $^1/_2$ cup)

Fresh rice cakes (*garaetteok*) 200 g
(7 oz)

Chilli paste seasoning

Onion $^1/_4$, peeled and grated, then
squeezed to extract juice

Korean chilli powder 1 Tbsp

Anchovy stock (see page 113) 2 Tbsp

Chilli paste 1 Tbsp

Minced garlic 1 tsp

Sesame oil 1 tsp

Chinese cooking wine (Shaoxing) 1 Tbsp

Sugar $^1/_2$ Tbsp

Salt a pinch

Ground black pepper a pinch

1   Cut fish cake and cabbage into 5-cm (2-in) slices. Set aside.

2   Combine ingredients for chili paste seasoning in a mixing bowl.

3   Heat oil in a frying pan over medium-high heat. Stir-fry leek, cabbage and fish cake slices for 3 minutes, then add anchovy stock and chilli paste seasoning. Stir to mix well, then add rice cakes. Stir to mix well, making sure ingredients are evenly coated with chilli paste seasoning. Leave mixture to simmer for 5–7 minutes.

4   Dish out and serve immediately.

Note: Korean fish cake may be substituted with any other type of fish cake. Frozen rice cakes may be used if fresh ones are not readily available.

sliced rice cakes in soup tteok guk

This is a festive dish that is traditionally served on the first day of the Korean new year as it is believed to symbolise good luck and longevity. However, it is delicious enough to eat on a daily basis! **Serves 4**

Frozen sliced rice cakes 200 g (7 oz)

Seaweed (*nori*) 2 sheets

Eggs 2

Beef brisket 300 g (11 oz)

Water 1.6 litres (52 fl oz / 6½ cups)

Salt to taste

Anchovy sauce 1 Tbsp

Minced garlic 1 tsp

Finely chopped leek 1 Tbsp, for garnish

Marinade (combined)

Salt 1 tsp

Finely chopped spring onion (scallion) 1 Tbsp

Minced garlic 1 tsp

Sesame oil 1 tsp

Ground black pepper a pinch

1   Soak frozen rice cakes in water for 10 minutes to thaw them. Drain well and set aside.

2   Cut seaweed into 5-cm (2-in) strips. Set aside. Make egg yolk and egg white omelettes (see page 54).

3   Cut beef brisket into 5-cm (2-in) pieces. Bring 1.6 litres (52 fl oz / 6½ cups) water to the boil. Add beef and increase to high heat. Skim off scum and impurities that rise to the surface, then reduce heat to low. Leave beef to cook for about 1 hour or until tender. Remove beef from heat and transfer to a bowl. Shred beef finely, then pour marinade over and mix well. Leave to marinate until needed.

4   Keep beef stock heated over low heat. Add salt, anchovy sauce and garlic. Add thawed rice cakes and increase heat to bring stock to the boil. Cook until rice cakes float to the surface and are tender.

5   Divide rice cake and stock among 4 serving bowls. Top with shredded beef, omelette and seaweed strips. Garnish with leek and serve immediately.

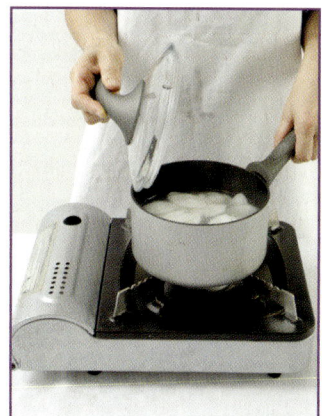

beef and vegetable hot stone rice bibimbap

Literally translated as "mixed rice", the variety, flavours and textures of the lightly seasoned vegetables in *bibimbap* make it a delicious, nutritionally balanced one-dish meal. **Serves 4**

Minced beef 200 g (7 oz)

Cooking oil as needed

Eggs 4

Cooked short-grain rice 200 g (7 oz)

Vegetables

Soy bean sprouts 300 g (11 oz)

Salt 1/2 tsp

Minced garlic 1 tsp

Sesame oil 1 Tbsp

Dried shiitake mushrooms 30 g (1 oz), soaked in water to soften

Japanese cucumbers 2, thinly sliced into 5-cm (2-in) strips

Carrot 1, peeled and sliced into 5-cm (2-in) strips

Beef marinade (combined)

Light soy sauce 1 Tbsp

Sugar 1 tsp

Sesame oil 1 Tbsp

Ground black pepper 1/4 tsp

Chilli paste seasoning (combined)

Korean chilli paste 4 Tbsp

Sugar 1 Tbsp

Glucose 1 Tbsp

Sesame oil 2 Tbsp

White sesame seeds a pinch

1 Place minced beef in a bowl with marinade. Leave until needed.

2 Prepare vegetables. Blanch soy bean sprouts for 1–2 minutes, then remove and drain. Season with salt, garlic and sesame oil. Set aside. Drain mushrooms. Remove stems and discard. Slice mushrooms into 1-cm (1/2-in) slices. Sprinkle some salt over cucumber strips. Leave for 10 minutes, then squeeze of excess water.

3 Heat some cooking oil in a frying pan over medium heat. Stir-fry mushrooms for 3 minutes. Season with salt, then remove and set aside. Add carrot and stir-fry for 3–5 minutes or until slightly tender. Remove and set aside. Add cucumbers and stir-fry for 1 minute. Reheat pan and stir-fry minced beef until cooked. Remove and set aside.

4 Lightly oil four traditional stone bowls or regular serving bowls. Divide cooked rice among bowls, then arrange minced beef and cooked vegetables in neat sections on top of rice, leaving a small space in the middle for a fried egg. Drizzle sesame oil over rice and vegetables, then heat stone bowls on stove top over medium heat for 5–7 minutes or until fragrant. Remove from heat and set aside. Skip this step if not using stone bowls.

5 Heat a little oil in a clean frying pan over medium heat and fry eggs sunny-side-up style. For a neater presentation, trim the edges of egg whites before placing in the centre of each rice portion.

6 To serve, garnish with sesame seeds. Chilli paste seasoning should be mixed in with rice and all the ingredients. Alternatively, serve it on the side and add as preferred.

raw fish and vegetables with rice hoedeopbap

This refreshing combination of tuna sashimi and vegetables with rice is perfect for a light lunch on a hot day. **Serves 4**

Sashimi-grade tuna 300 g (11 oz)

Red cabbage leaves 2

Carrot 1/2

Japanese cucumber 1

White radish 1/3

Iceberg lettuce 8 leaves

Cooked short-grain rice 200 g (7 oz)

Garlic 4 cloves, peeled and finely sliced

Sesame oil 1 Tbsp

Sliced red and green chillies (optional)
for garnish

Chilli paste seasoning (combined)

Korean chilli paste 3 Tbsp

Sugar 1 Tbsp

White rice vinegar 1 Tbsp

Finely chopped spring onion (scallion)
1 Tbsp

Freshly squeezed lemon juice 1 1/2 Tbsp

White sesame seeds a pinch

1   Using a sharp knife, cut tuna into 1-cm (1/2-in) cubes. Refrigerate until needed.

2   Slice cabbage, carrot, cucumber and radish into 5-cm (2-in) strips. Shred lettuce leaves finely. Place vegetables separately in iced water. Leave for about 10 minutes, then drain and refrigerate until needed.

3   To assemble dish, divide rice among 4 serving bowls. Arrange shredded lettuce in a layer over rice, then place sliced vegetables and garlic in neat sections on top. Place tuna in the middle of rice, then drizzle sesame oil over.

4   Garnish with chilli slices, if desired and serve immediately with chilli paste seasoning on the side. To eat, pour chilli paste seasoning over rice and mix with all the ingredients.

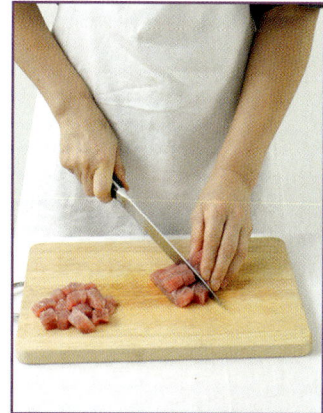

meat and poultry

simmered chicken 73

sweet fried chicken 74

boiled pork belly 77

stir-fried pork 78

simmered pork ribs 81

simmered ox tail 82

stir-fried beef 85

simmered chicken dakgogi jorim

This flavourful simmered dish is quick and easy to prepare. **Serves 4**

Whole chicken 1, about 1 kg (1 lb 1½ oz), cut into serving sizes

Salt to taste

Ground black pepper to taste

Potatoes 2, peeled

Carrot ½, peeled

Onion 1, peeled

Fresh shiitake mushrooms 4

Cooking oil ½ Tbsp

Water 125 ml (4 fl oz / ½ cup)

White sesame seeds a pinch

Radish sprouts a handful

Marinade (combined)

Light soy sauce 125 ml (4 fl oz / ½ cup)

Sugar 3 Tbsp

Finely chopped spring onion (scallion) 3 Tbsp

Minced garlic 2 Tbsp

Grated ginger 1 Tbsp

Chinese cooking wine (Shaoxing) 1 Tbsp

Ground black pepper a pinch

Korean chilli paste 1 Tbsp

Korean chilli powder 1 Tbsp

1   Rub chicken evenly with salt and pepper. Set aside.

2   Cut potatoes and carrot into 2.5-cm (1-in) cubes. Slice onion thinly. Wipe caps and remove stems from mushrooms. Set aside.

3   Heat a frying pan over medium-high heat. Without using any oil, sear chicken evenly for 5–7 minutes until turn light golden brown all over. Set aside.

4   Heat cooking oil in a clean saucepan over medium heat. Stir-fry potatoes, carrot, onion and mushrooms for 3–5 minutes or until slightly tender, then remove and set aside. Reheat pan and add chicken, half of marinade and water. Increase heat slightly and bring to the boil. Leave to boil for 10 minutes.

5   Return potato mixture to pan, then add remaining marinade. Allow mixture to boil for 5–7 minutes, then reduce heat slightly and leave to simmer for 10 more minutes, or until chicken is tender and liquid has reduced to a thick gravy.

6   Dish out and garnish with sesame seeds and radish sprouts. Serve hot with plain white rice.

Note: Searing the chicken seals in the juices, thus retaining the chicken's flavour and moisture that may be lost during the simmering process, preventing the chicken from becoming tough and tasteless.

sweet fried chicken dak gang jung

Coated in a delightful sweet-savoury sauce, these fried chicken wings make a great snack, and are especially popular with children. **Serves 4**

Chicken wings 1.5 kg (3 lb 4½ oz), wing and drumsticks separated

Corn flour (cornstarch) 4 Tbsp

Plain (all-purpose) flour 4 Tbsp

Cooking oil as needed

Mixed salad greens (optional) a handful

Marinade (combined)

Onion ½, peeled

Light soy sauce ½ Tbsp

Grated ginger 1 Tbsp

Chinese cooking wine (Shaoxing) 1 Tbsp

Salt 1–2 pinches

Ground black pepper 1–2 pinches

Sweet sauce

Cooking oil 1 Tbsp

Minced garlic 1 Tbsp

Grated ginger 1 tsp

Light soy sauce 2 Tbsp

Sesame oil 1 tsp

White sesame seeds 1 Tbsp

Fresh apple juice 1 Tbsp

Glucose 2 Tbsp

Honey 3 Tbsp

Korean chilli paste ½ Tbsp

1 Place a flat grater over a small bowl. Grate onion and squeeze to extract juice. Combine with remaining marinade ingredients.

2 Place chicken wings in a bowl. Pour marinade over chicken wings while rubbing it into the meat. Leave to marinate for at least 30 minutes.

3 Heat about 750 ml (24 fl oz / 3 cups) cooking oil in a frying pan over medium-high heat. While oil is heating, combine both types of flour in a deep plate. Coat chicken wings in flour mixture evenly.

4 Fry chicken wings in batches, cooking each batch for 5–7 minutes or until cooked and golden brown. Add more oil as needed. To test if chicken wings are cooked, prick the fleshiest part with a fork or bamboo skewer. If juices run clear, the wings are cooked. Drain chicken wings and set aside.

5 Keep pan heated. Prepare sweet sauce. Heat oil and fry garlic until fragrant. Add remaining ingredients for sweet sauce and mix well. Bring mixture to the boil, then return chicken wings to the pan. Coat wings evenly with sweet sauce.

6 Dish out and serve immediately, with salad greens on the side, if desired.

boiled pork belly soo yook

The fat from the pork belly is rendered while it is gently simmered in a flavourful broth, making this dish slightly less sinful. Serve as a main dish or appetiser. **Serves 4**

Pork belly 500 g (1 lb 1½ oz)

Water 2 litres (64 fl oz / 8 cups)

Fermented soy bean paste 3 Tbsp

Onion 1, peeled

Ginger 10 g (⅓ oz), peeled

Instant coffee powder 1 Tbsp

Cinnamon sticks 10 g (⅓ oz)

Sauce (combined)

Korean preserved prawns (shrimps)
1 Tbsp

White rice vinegar ½ Tbsp

Water 1 Tbsp

Chili powder ½ tsp

White sesame seeds 1 tsp

Finely chopped spring onion (scallion)
1 Tbsp

1   Slice pork belly into half lengthwise. Set aside.

2   Combine water, soy bean paste, onion, ginger, coffee powder and cinnamon in a pot. Bring to the boil over high heat, then add pork belly. Reduce heat to medium-low and leave to cook for 30 minutes or until pork belly is tender.

3   Remove pork belly from pot. Wrap pork tightly with plastic wrap, then set aside to cool. When cool, unwrap and slice into 0.5-cm (¼-in) slices.

4   Arrange pork belly slices on a serving platter. Drizzle sauce over and serve immediately.

stir-fried pork dwaeji bulgogi

This is a pork variation of the popular *bulgogi*. **Serves 4**

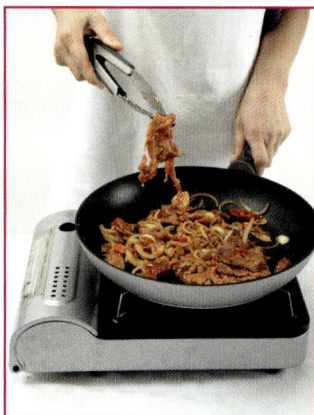

Onion 1

Green and red chillies 2 each, or more
if a spicier flavour is desired

Garlic 3 cloves, peeled and sliced

Finely chopped spring onion (scallion)
2 tsp

Grated ginger 2 tsp

Light soy sauce 2 Tbsp

Sugar 2 Tbsp

Pear juice 3 Tbsp or grate $^1/_2$ Korean pear
and squeeze to extract 3 Tbsp juice

White sesame seeds 2 tsp

Ground black pepper a pinch

Sesame oil 2 tsp

Pork 300 g (11 oz), thinly sliced

Cooking oil as needed

Korean chilli paste 2 Tbsp

1   Peel onion and cut into half. Trim off and discard about 0.5-cm ($^1/_4$-in)
    off the ends of both halves. Slice onion thinly. Set aside.

2   Trim off stalks from chillies, then slice them on the diagonal. Remove the
    seeds, if desired.

3   Combine sliced chillies, garlic, spring onion, grated ginger, soy sauce,
    sugar, pear juice, sesame seeds, black pepper and sesame oil in a mixing
    bowl and mix well. Add pork and leave to marinate.

4   Heat a little cooking oil in a frying pan over medium-high heat. Stir-fry
    onion until fragrant, then add marinated pork slices and stir-fry quickly
    for 3–5 minutes or until pork is cooked.

5   Dish out and serve hot with plain white rice.

simmered pork ribs dwaeji galbi jjim

These pork ribs are tenderly succulent right down to the last bite. **Serves 4**

Dried shiitake mushrooms 8, soaked in water to soften

Pork ribs 1 kg (1 lb 1½ oz) cut into short lengths

Carrot 1, peeled

Potatoes 2, peeled

Red and green chillies 2 each

Water 125 ml (4 fl oz / ½ cup)

Marinade (combined)

Light soy sauce 150 ml (5⅓ fl oz)

Water 150 ml (5⅓ fl oz)

Sugar 4 tsp

Onion ½, peeled and finely chopped

Finely minced garlic 3 tsp

Grated ginger 1 tsp

Ground black pepper a pinch

Sesame oil 1 Tbsp

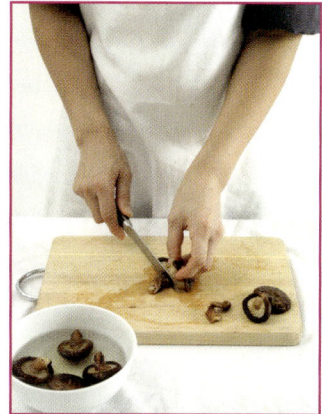

1. Cut off and discard mushroom stems.

2. Trim fat from pork ribs. Place ribs in a basin of water and leave to soak for 10 minutes to remove impurities.

3. Meanwhile, cut carrot and potatoes into 2.5-cm (1-in) cubes. Slice chillies on the diagonal.

4. Drain pork ribs. Heat a frying pan over medium-high heat. When pan is very hot, sear pork ribs until any remaining fat is rendered. Remove and place in a bowl.

5. Add marinade to pork ribs and mix well. Leave to marinate for 1 hour.

6. Place pork ribs and marinade in a pot. Add water and bring to the boil over medium-high heat, then reduce heat and leave to simmer until cooking liquid has reduced by half.

7. Add mushrooms, carrot, potatoes and chillies and return mixture to the boil. Leave to cook for 20 minutes or until vegetables and pork ribs are tender and cooking liquid has reduced and thickened into a gravy.

8. Dish out and garnish as desired. Serve hot.

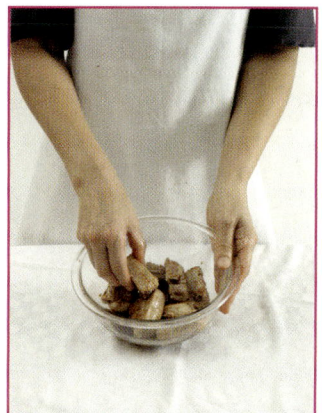

simmered ox tail ggori jjim

Ox tail meat is surprisingly tender and flavourful. It is a real treat. **Serves 4**

Green and red capsicums (bell peppers)
  1 each

Ox tail 600 g (1 lb 5$^1/_3$ oz)

Water 375 ml (12 fl oz / 1$^1/_2$ cups)

Chestnuts 5, peeled and cut into
  2.5-cm (1-in) pieces

Carrot $^1/_2$, cut into 2.5-cm (1-in) pieces

Dried shiitake mushrooms 5, soaked in
  water to soften

White radish $^1/_4$, cut into 2.5-cm (1-in)
  rounds

Marinade (combined)

Light soy sauce 4 Tbsp

Sesame oil 1 Tbsp

Sugar $^1/_2$ Tbsp

Glucose 2 Tbsp

Pear juice 125 ml (4 fl oz / $^1/_2$ cup) or
  grate 1 Korean pear and squeeze to
  extract 125 ml (4 fl oz / $^1/_2$ cup) juice

Minced garlic 1 Tbsp

Grated ginger 1 tsp

Chinese cooking wine (Shaoxing) 1 Tbsp

White sesame seeds $^1/_2$ Tbsp

Ground black pepper $^1/_4$ tsp

Finely chopped spring onion (scallion)
  2 Tbsp

1 Slice capsicums in half. Using your hands or a knife, remove the white pith and seeds. Slice capsicums into thick strips and set aside.

2 Cut ox tail into 5-cm (2-in) pieces, then trim fat. Blanch ox tail in a pot of boiling water for 1–2 minutes or until impurities rise to the surface. Remove and drain, then transfer to a bowl. Pour marinade over ox tail and mix well. Leave to marinate for 30 minutes.

3 Place water and all other ingredients except capsicums in a pot and bring to the boil over medium-high heat. Add ox tail, then reduce heat and leave to simmer for 1 hour or until ox tail is tender and cooking liquid has reduced and thickened to a gravy.

4 Add capsicums and cook until slightly tender before removing from heat.

5 Dish out, garnish as desired and serve hot.

stir-fried beef bulgogi

Bulgogi is one of Korea's most popular barbecued meat dishes. This stir-fried version does not compromise on flavour and is every bit as delicious. **Serves 4**

Beef sirloin or tenderloin 500 g
(1 lb 1 1/2 oz)

Garlic 1 bulb, cloves peeled and separated

Golden mushrooms a handful, cleaned
and blanched in hot water for
1–2 minutes

Iceberg or butterhead lettuce
10–15 leaves

Carrot 1/2, peeled and sliced into strips

Cooking oil as needed

Finely chopped spring onion (scallion)
1 Tbsp

Marinade (combined)

Light soy sauce 4 Tbsp

Sugar 2 Tbsp

Pear juice 4 Tbsp or grate 1 Korean pear
and squeeze to extract 4 Tbsp juice

Finely chopped spring onion (scallion)
3 Tbsp

Minced garlic 1 1/2 Tbsp

Ground black pepper 1 tsp

Sesame oil 1 1/2 Tbsp

Dipping sauce

Fermented soy bean paste 2 Tbsp

Korean chilli paste 1 Tbsp

Minced garlic 1/2 tsp

Sesame oil 1/2 tsp

White sesame seeds a pinch

Mayonnaise 1 tsp

1 Slice beef thinly, then place in a bowl with marinade. Mix well and leave for at least 30 minutes. If a stronger flavour is preferred, beef can be marinated a day in advance and kept refrigerated until needed.

2 Heat a frying pan over medium-high heat. Without using oil, fry garlic cloves until fragrant and slightly golden brown. Remove and set aside.

3 Bring a pot of water to the boil and blanch mushrooms for 1–2 minutes or until just tender. Remove and set aside. Arrange lettuce, carrot strips and garlic cloves on a serving plate and set aside.

4 Heat a little cooking oil in a frying pan over medium-high heat. Stir-fry beef slices until cooked to medium or medium-well doneness. Remove and transfer to a serving plate.

5 Prepare dipping sauce. Combine soy bean paste, chilli paste, garlic, sesame and sesame seeds and mix well. Stir in mayonnaise. Transfer sauce to a sauce dish.

6 Stir-fried beef can be served in two ways: garnished with spring onions and mushrooms and served hot with plain white rice, or made into lettuce wraps. To make lettuce wraps, place a few slices of beef, carrot strips and garlic cloves on a lettuce leaf. Drizzle some dipping sauce over beef, then wrap lettuce up tightly to enclose the filling.

soups and stews

soy bean paste stew 88

spicy bean curd stew 91

seaweed soup 92

ginseng chicken soup 95

spicy chicken soup 96

spicy beef soup 99

beef rib soup 100

soy bean paste stew doenjang jigae

This hearty, nutritious bean curd stew is laced with the sweetness of clams and spiciness of kimchi. Omit the chillies for a non-spicy version. **Serves 4**

Short-neck clams 100 g (3^1/$_2$ oz)

Salt as needed

Courgette (zucchini) ^{1}/$_2$

Silken bean curd 100 g (3^1/$_2$ oz)

Fresh shiitake mushrooms 4

Anchovy stock (see page 113) 800 ml (26^2/$_3$ fl oz / 3^1/$_4$ cups)

Fermented soy bean paste 3 Tbsp

Leek ^{1}/$_2$, ends trimmed and sliced thinly on the diagonal

Red and green chillies 1 each, sliced

Minced garlic 1 tsp

Korean chilli powder 2 tsp

1   Place clams in a large bowl. Fill with enough water to cover clams, then add a heaped tablespoonful of salt. Leave to soak for 30 minutes for clams to expel sand and dirt. Remove clams carefully so as not to agitate any sand at the bottom of the bowl. Rinse under running water, drain and set aside.

2   Slice courgette into half lengthwise, then cut into 1-cm (^{1}/$_2$-in) pieces. Slice bean curd into 1-cm (^{1}/$_2$-in) cubes. Slice mushroom caps in half. Set aside.

3   In a pot, bring anchovy stock to the boil over medium heat. Strain soy bean paste into the boiling stock through a fine mesh sieve.

4   Add courgette, mushrooms and bean curd to pot. Cook until courgette is tender, then add clams, stirring gently. Clams should begin to open while cooking in the heat. Discard any clams that remain closed. Add leek, chillies, garlic and chilli powder and mix well.

5   Dish out and serve immediately.

spicy bean curd stew sundubu jigae

This rich-tasting, savoury stew is perfect with plain white rice. **Serves 4**

Short-neck clams 150 g (5¹/₃ oz)

Pork 150 g (5¹/₃ oz)

Sesame oil ¹/₂ Tbsp

Sugar a pinch

Minced garlic 1 tsp

Grated ginger 1 tsp

Ground black pepper a pinch

Vegetable oil 2 Tbsp

Korean chilli powder 2 Tbsp

Cabbage kimchi (see page 42) 100 g
(3¹/₂ oz), cut into 2.5-cm (1-in) lengths

Red chilli 1, coarsely sliced

Anchovy stock (see page 113) 500 ml
(16 fl oz / 2 cups)

Round silken bean curd 500 g
(1 lb 1¹/₂ oz), sliced into rounds

Salt a pinch

Seasoning (combined)

Light soy sauce 2 Tbsp

Korean chilli powder 1 tsp

Sesame oil ¹/₂ Tbsp

Finely chopped spring onion (scallion)
1 tsp

Minced garlic 1 tsp

1 Prepare clams (see page 88). While clams are soaking, slice pork into
   1-cm (¹/₂-in) pieces. Place in a bowl and marinate with sesame oil, sugar,
   garlic, grated ginger and pepper. Leave to marinate until needed.

2 Heat oil in a pot over medium heat. When oil is hot, add chilli powder
   and mix well, then add pork, kimchi and chilli. Stir-fry for 3–4 minutes
   or until pork is cooked.

3 Add clams and anchovy stock. Increase heat slightly and bring mixture
   to the boil. Add bean curd slices by sliding the pieces gently into the pot,
   being careful not to break them up. Add seasoning and stir gently to
   mix well. Reduce heat and simmer until clams open up. Discard any
   unopened clams.

4 Dish out and serve hot with plain white rice.

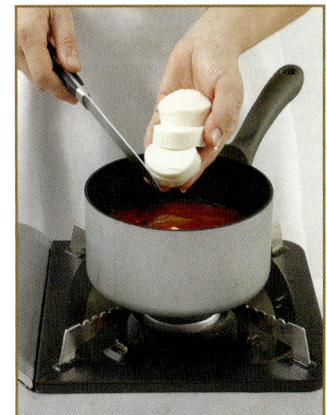

seaweed soup miyeok guk

Quick and easy to make, this soup is rich in calcium and nutrients. It is typically consumed by expectant and nursing mothers in Korea. Seafood may also be used in place of beef, if preferred. **Serves 4**

Dried seaweed (*wakame*) 20 g (²/₃ oz)

Water 2.5 litres (80 fl oz / 10 cups)

Beef brisket 300 g (11 oz)

Onion 1, peeled

Coarse black pepper 1 Tbsp

Minced garlic 1 tsp

Sesame oil 1 Tbsp

Anchovy sauce 2 Tbsp

Salt to taste

1 Soak seaweed in a bowl of water for 5–10 minutes. Seaweed should expand into large sheets. Rinse seaweed, then drain and slice into 4-cm (1¹/₂-in) lengths. Set aside.

2 In a pot, bring water to the boil over medium heat. Add beef, onion and pepper. Leave to cook for 1–2 hours or until stock has reduced by almost half and beef is tender. Remove from heat and set aside. Drain beef and leave to cool.

3 Heat another pot over medium heat. Add seaweed, garlic, sesame oil and anchovy sauce and stir-fry for 5 minutes, mixing well. Add beef stock and mix well. Cover pot and bring to the boil. Leave boiling for 30 minutes.

4 Shred beef finely, then add to pot. Boil for another 5 minutes, then season with salt to taste.

5 Dish out and serve immediately. Garnish as desired.

ginseng chicken soup sam gye tang

This hearty, warming dish is traditionally eaten in the summer in Korea, as it is believed that the warming qualities of chicken and ginseng help to rid the body of toxins through perspiration. Serve as a main dish. **Serves 4**

Chicken 1 whole, 600–700 g
(1 lb 5^1/$_3$ oz–1^1/$_2$ oz)

Glutinous (sticky) rice 70 g (2^1/$_2$ oz /
^{1}/$_3$ cup), soaked in water for 2 hours

Garlic 8–10 cloves, peeled

Dried red dates 4

Korean dried ginseng 2, soaked in water
for 3–4 hours

Salt to taste

1 Prepare chicken. Clean chicken and discard organs. Cut off and discard head, feet, wing tips and neck. Rinse chicken thoroughly.

2 Drain glutinous rice and stuff it into the cavity of the chicken, together with garlic cloves. Seal cavity by skewering 1–2 toothpicks through the skin.

3 Place chicken in a big pot. Pour in enough water to cover chicken, then add red dates and ginseng. Bring to the boil over high heat. Skim off scum and impurities that rise to the surface, then reduce heat and leave to simmer for 1 hour or until chicken is tender. Remove toothpicks from chicken.

4 Serve hot with a small saucer of salt on the side for seasoning to taste.

spicy chicken soup dak gae jang

This flavourful soup is only lightly spicy, and may be suitable for palates that are not accustomed to spice. Reduce the amount of chilli powder as preferred. **Serves 4**

Chicken 1 whole, 1–1.5 kg
  (2 lb 3 oz–1 lb 4½ oz)

Water 2 litres (64 fl oz / 8 cups)

Onion 1, peeled

Korean chilli powder 2 Tbsp

Sesame oil 2 Tbsp

Minced garlic 3 Tbsp

Anchovy sauce 2 Tbsp

Ground black pepper a pinch

Chinese cooking wine (Shaoxing) 1 Tbsp

Leeks 3

Salt to taste

1   Place chicken, water and onion in a large pot. Bring to the boil over high heat, skimming off scum and impurities that rise to the surface. Reduce heat and leave to simmer for 1 hour or until chicken is tender. Remove chicken and discard onion, reserving stock. Shred chicken meat coarsely, discarding skin and bones.

2   Place shredded chicken meat in a mixing bowl. Add chilli powder, sesame oil, garlic, anchovy sauce, pepper and cooking wine. Mix well and set aside.

3   Trim leeks and slice into 5-cm (2-in) lengths. Cut each length further into half lengthwise. Bring a pot of water to the boil. Blanch leeks for 30 seconds to 1 minute, then remove and rinse with cold water immediately. Set leeks aside.

4   Reheat reserved stock over medium heat. Skim off excess oil, then add shredded chicken meat and blanched leeks. Bring to the boil for 10 minutes, then season with salt to taste.

5   Dish out and serve hot.

spicy beef soup yuk gae jang

This soup is redolent with the robust taste of beef and the subtle flavours of leeks and *gosari* (bracken fern). **Serves 4**

Beef sirloin 600 g (1 lb 5¹/₃ oz)

Water as needed

Dried bracken fern 30 g (1 oz)

Leeks 3, ends trimmed and sliced into 10-cm (4-in) lengths

Chinese (napa) cabbage 200 g (7 oz), sliced into 10-cm (4-in) lengths

Soy bean sprouts 200 g (7 oz)

Korean chilli powder 2 Tbsp

Sesame oil 2 Tbsp

Minced garlic 3 Tbsp

Anchovy sauce or light soy sauce 2 Tbsp

Ground black pepper a pinch

Salt to taste

1   Trim fat from beef, then soak in water to remove impurities (see page 100).

2   Prepare dried bracken fern. Soak fern in a bowl of water for 1 hour. Bring a pot of water to the boil over medium-low heat. Add fern and boil for 40 minutes. Remove, then rinse in cold water and drain. Cut into short, evenly-sized lengths and set aside.

3   In a pot, bring 4 litres (128 fl oz / 16 cups) water to the boil over medium heat. Add beef and leave to cook for 1 hour or until tender. Remove beef and set aside to cool, reserving stock. Shred beef coarsely. Set aside.

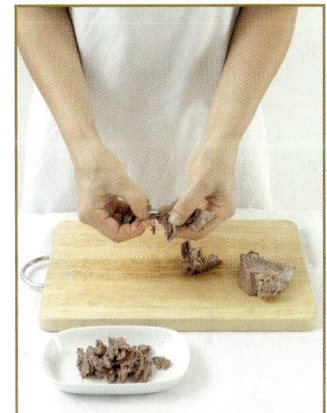

4   Bring a pot of water to the boil. Add leeks, cabbage and soy bean sprouts and cook for 5 minutes, then remove and place in a colander. Rinse vegetables under running water, then drain and squeeze to remove excess water. Set aside.

5   Combine chilli powder and sesame oil in a mixing bowl. Add cooked vegetables, bracken fern, shredded beef, garlic, anchovy sauce or light soy sauce and pepper. Mix well.

6   Reheat reserved stock over medium heat. Add seasoned mixture and bring to the boil for 20 minutes. Season with salt to taste.

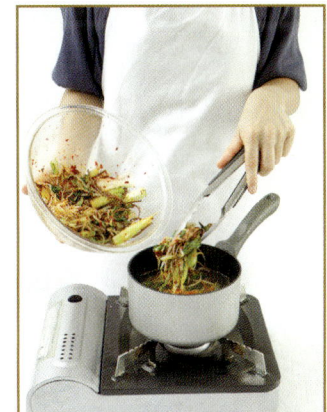

7   Dish out and serve hot.

beef rib soup galbitang

This dish has its roots in the 18th century, when it was served to Korean royalty. These days, it is popularly enjoyed by everyone in Korea. **Serves 4**

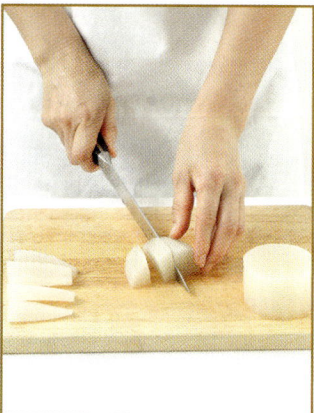

Beef short ribs 1.5 kg (3 lb 4$^1/_2$ oz)

Water as needed

White radish 500 g (1 lb 1$^1/_2$ oz), peeled and cut into large chunks

Onion 1, peeled

Garlic 10 cloves, peeled

Leeks 2, ends trimmed and sliced into 5-cm (2-in) lengths

Black peppercorns 1 Tbsp

Dried sweet potato vermicelli 100 g (3$^1/_2$ oz)

Salt 2 Tbsp

Beef seasoning powder 1 Tbsp

Garnish

Finely chopped spring onions (scallions) 100 g (3$^1/_2$ oz)

Minced garlic 2 Tbsp (optional)

1 Trim fat from beef ribs, then cut into 5-cm (2-in) lengths. Place in a large bowl and add enough water to cover. Leave to soak for 20 minutes to remove impurities, then rinse under running water and drain.

2 Bring a pot of water to the boil. Add beef ribs and cook for 7–10 minutes or until impurities rise to the surface. Remove ribs and rinse under running water. Set aside.

3 Bring 4 litres (128 fl oz / 16 cups) water to the boil in a large pot over.; medium-high heat. Add beef ribs, radish, onion, garlic, leeks and peppercorns. Cook for 40 minutes, then remove vegetables, discarding onion, garlic and leeks. Slice radish into 5-cm (2-in) lengths. Set vegetables aside. Continue to cook beef ribs for another hour or until tender.

4 Bring another pot of water to the boil. Blanch vermicelli briefly until softened, then remove and drain. Using a pair of scissors, cut noodles into short lengths, approximately 5–8 cm (2–3 in).

5 Add salt and beef seasoning powder to pot of beef and stir to mix well. Return radish to the pot and cook for another 10 minutes.

6 Divide noodles, beef ribs and radish among 4 serving bowls. Ladle soup over and garnish with spring onions and minced garlic, if using. Serve immediately.

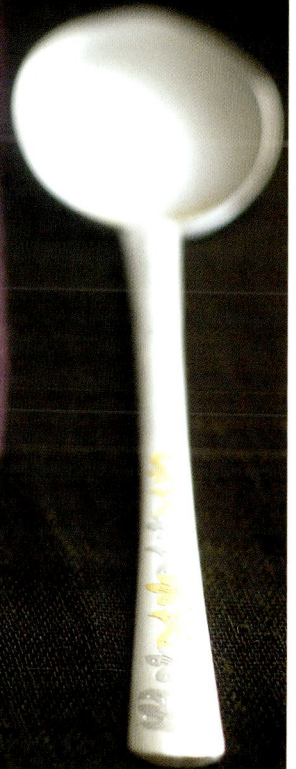

desserts

sweetened glutinous rice 104

cinnamon punch 107

sweet pumpkin porridge 108

sweetened apple fritters 111

sweetened glutinous rice yak sik

This classic Korean rice snack is traditionally served during Daeboreum, a Korean holiday that celebrates the first full moon in the Korean lunar calendar. **Serves 4**

Glutinous (sticky) rice 630 g (1 lb 6 oz / 3 cups)

Water as needed

Dried red dates 15

Chestnuts 10

Light soy sauce 3 Tbsp

Dark soy sauce 1 tsp

Sesame oil 4 Tbsp

Brown sugar 20 g ($^2/_3$ oz)

Pine nuts 1 Tbsp

Ground cinnamon $^1/_2$ Tbsp

1 Prepare glutinous rice a few hours ahead. Rinse and drain glutinous rice, then place in a bowl. Add enough water to cover rice and leave to soak for 4–5 hours.

2 Slice red dates lengthwise, leaving the core in the centre. Discard core. Peel chestnuts, then cut into 1-cm ($^1/_2$-in) pieces. Set aside.

3 Drain glutinous rice and place in a mixing bowl.

4 Combine light and dark soy sauces, 3 Tbsp sesame oil and sugar and mix well. Add this seasoning and the chestnuts to glutinous rice and mix well.

5 Place glutinous rice mixture in a pressure cooker and add 500 ml (16 fl oz / 2 cups) water. Cover and cook over high heat. When steam starts to emerge from the cooker, turn it off and leave for 5 minutes or until steam dissipates. Remove glutinous rice from cooker and add remaining sesame oil, red dates, pine nuts and ground cinnamon and mix well.

6 Pack glutinous rice mixture tightly into a medium-size square or rectangular container 5-cm (2-in) deep. Leave to cool to room temperature before slicing into serving portions and serving.

cinnamon punch su jeong gwa

This refreshing drink is redolent with the sweetness of dried persimmons, and is best enjoyed on a hot day. **Serves 4**

Mature ginger 30 g (1 oz)

Dried persimmons 3

Walnuts 3

Water 2 litres (64 fl oz / 8 cups)

Cinnamon sticks 40 g (1⅓ oz)

Brown sugar 250 g (9 oz)

1   Peel ginger, then slice into 0.5-cm (¼-in) slices. Set aside.

2   Slice persimmons, spreading them out flat. Place a walnut on one side of a sliced persimmon and roll up tightly. Repeat for remaining persimmons and walnuts. Slice stuffed persimmon rolls into 4 pieces each and set aside.

3   In a pot, bring water to the boil over medium heat. Add ginger and cinnamon sticks, then reduce heat and leave to simmer for 40 minutes.

4   Remove ginger and cinnamon sticks, then add sugar, stirring until sugar is completely dissolved. Remove from heat. Leave mixture to cool, then refrigerate to chill. Add persimmon pieces before serving.

sweet pumpkin porridge ho bak juk

This classic Korean dessert has a rich, velvety texture. **Serves 4**

Glutinous (sticky) rice 2 Tbsp

Water as needed

Pumpkin 1, about 500 g (1 lb 1$^{1}/_{2}$ oz)

Sugar 2 Tbsp

Salt $^{1}/_{2}$ tsp

Pine nuts 2 tsp

Red dates a handful, sliced

1 Soak glutinous rice with 125 ml (4 fl oz / $^{1}/_{2}$ cup) water for 1 hour. In a blender, blend glutinous rice with the soaking liquid until fine. Set aside.

2 Cut pumpkin in half, then remove seeds by scraping with a spoon. Peel pumpkin, then slice into 1-cm ($^{1}/_{2}$-in) pieces.

3 Combine pumpkin with 400 ml (13$^{1}/_{3}$ fl oz /1$^{2}/_{3}$ cups) water in a pot and bring to the boil for 20 minutes over low heat or until pumpkin is tender. Transfer pumpkin and boiling water to a blender and process into a smooth paste.

4 Transfer blended pumpkin to a pot. Add blended glutinous rice mixture and heat over low heat. Stir continuously for 10 minutes or until pumpkin porridge is smooth with a thickened consistency. Add sugar and salt and mix well.

5 Serve hot or chilled, garnished with pine nuts and red dates.

sweetened apple fritters sa gwa jeong gwa

This dessert is popular with both children and adults, and is a great way to use up leftover apples. **Serves 4**

Apples 2

Dried red dates 3

Water 200 ml (7 fl oz / $^4/_5$ cup)

Cinnamon sticks 20 g ($^2/_3$ oz)

Sugar 125 g ($4^1/_2$ oz / $^1/_2$ cup)

Salt a pinch

Glucose or honey 125 ml (4 fl oz / $^1/_2$ cup)

Lemon juice 1 Tbsp

Fresh cranberries (optional) 3–5

Fresh ginkgo nuts (optional) 3–5

1 Slice tops off apples and discard. Cut apples into quarters, then remove core.

2 Split red dates, then spread them out. Remove the core. Roll dates up and slice thinly.

3 Place water and cinnamon sticks in a saucepan and bring to the boil. Boil for 10 minutes, then remove cinnamon sticks and set aside.

4 Add sugar, salt, glucose or honey, lemon juice and apple slices to pan. Stir to mix well. Return water to the boil and leave boiling for another 10–15 minutes or until the boiling liquid reduces to a thick syrup and apple slices are tender. Ensure that apple slices are evenly coated with syrup. Remove from heat and leave apples to cool in pan for about 20 minutes. Add cranberries and gingko nuts to pan, if using.

5 Transfer apples to serving plates. Drizzle syrup over and garnish with sliced red dates, cinnamon sticks, cranberries and gingko nuts, if using. Serve warm.

basic recipes

anchovy stock

Makes about 2.5 litres (80 fl oz / 10 cups)

Water 3 litres (96 fl oz / 12 cups)

Korean dried anchovies 20 g ($^2/_3$ oz)

Onion 100 g ($3^1/_2$ oz), peeled

Kelp 10 g ($^1/_3$ oz), wiped clean

Leeks 2, ends trimmed, chopped

1 Combine all ingredients in a large pot and bring to the boil over medium heat. Skim off impurities that rise to the surface. Leave to boil for 30 minutes, then remove from heat, strain and discard ingredients.

2 If not using immediately, leave stock to cool, then refrigerate for up to 3 days or freeze for 15–20 days. Defrost over low heat or in the microwave oven when needed.

beef stock

Makes about 3 litres (96 fl oz / 12 cups)

Beef brisket or any preferred cut of beef 400 g ($14^1/_3$ oz)

Water 3 litres (96 fl oz / 12 cups)

Black peppercorns 1 Tbsp

Onion 100 g ($3^1/_2$ oz), peeled

1 Place beef in a bowl. Pour in enough water to cover and leave to soak 20 minutes to remove impurities. Rinse beef and drain.

2 Place beef in a large pot with 3 litres (96 fl oz / 12 cups) water, peppercorns and onion. Bring to the boil over high heat. Skim off impurities that rise to the surface, then reduce heat and leave to simmer for 1 hour.

3 Strain stock and discard peppercorns and onion. The beef brisket can be consumed or used in other dishes. If not using stock immediately, leave to cool, then refrigerate up to 3 days or freeze for 15–20 days. Defrost over low heat or in the microwave oven when needed.

glossary

1

3

5

2

4

6

1. Anchovies, dried

Korean anchovies are significantly larger and more flavourful than the common dried anchovies that are typically used in other Asian cuisines. They are consumed as a side dish or used to make stock. They can be substituted with the common variety of anchovies, although the flavour will not be as robust or satisfying.

2. Anchovy sauce

Known as *myulchi aekjot* in Korean, Korean anchovy sauce is saltier, with a more intense flavour as compared to other Southeast Asian varieties of fish sauce. Anchovy sauce is available in Korean supermarkets.

3. Dried bracken fern

Known as *gosari* in Korean, dried bracken ferns are a typical ingredient in *bibimbap*. In Korea, they are harvested during springtime, then preserved through salting, pickling or sun-drying.

4. Beef stock granules

Also known as beef bouillon powder, beef stock granules add an intense flavour to soups and stocks. Koreans use this ingredient sparingly, so as not to overpower the natural flavours of the soup or stock.

5. Brown rice vinegar

Brown rice vinegar is comparatively milder and less acidic compared to vinegars made from grains and alcohol. It is valued for its medicinal properties and adds a piquant flavour to dishes.

6. Korean chilli powder

Korean chilli powder is made from grinding dried red chillies into a powder. The chilli powder ranges from coarse to fine varieties.

7. Cinnamon

This spice has many culinary uses. It is valued for its subtly sweet flavour. Cinnamon is sold either in ground powder form or as whole sticks.

7

9

11

8

10

12

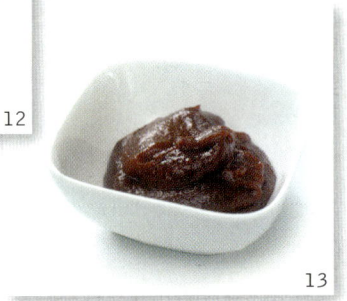
13

8. Glucose

This thick, clear syrup is available from Asian supermarkets. It has a consistency similar to that of honey, but with a milder sweetness. Corn syrup may be used if glucose is unavailable.

9. Dried shiitake mushrooms

Dried shiitake mushrooms feature heavily in many Asian cuisines. They are valued not just for their flavour, but medicinal properties. Dried shiitake mushrooms are preferred over fresh ones when a stronger flavour is desired. Soak for about 30 minutes to soften before using. The hard stem is usually trimmed off and discarded.

10. Korean dried ginseng

Ginseng is a highly prized ingredient in the realm of Korean cuisine. Aromatic, with a slightly bitter, medicinal taste, Koreans believe it has restorative properties for the body. There are different varieties of ginseng, graded according to quality.

11. Glutinous (sticky) rice

Also known as sticky rice, glutinous rice is a variety of short-grain rice that becomes sticky when cooked, due to a high starch content. In Korean cooking, it is employed in main dishes and desserts alike.

12. Kelp

Edible kelp is better known as *kombu*. It used to flavour stocks and has a high amount of glutamic acid, which gives the savoury element known as *umami* in Japanese. *Kombu* can be purchased readily from Japanese supermarkets.

13. Korean chilli paste

Also known as *gochujang*, Korean chilli paste is made from fermenting chilli powder, glutinous rice powder, fermented soy beans and salt together. It cannot be replaced with other types of chilli paste, as the resulting taste will be different. Commonly used in Korean cooking, it is easily available from Korean supermarkets.

14

16

18

15

17

19

14. Korean mustard

Korean mustard is spicy and usually sold in tubes. It can be used in dressings.

15. Korean preserved prawns (shrimps)

These preserved prawns are different because they are larger in size and much sweeter than the common Asian variety. Hence, they are usually not substituted.

16. Leeks

Leeks feature heavily in Korean cooking as it is enjoyed for its mild, onion-like flavour. The dark green portion is usually discarded since it has less flavour, and can be woody and very chewy if the leek is mature. Leeks are used to flavour soups, added to stir-fries and used to make kimchi.

17. Lotus root

Lotus roots are the roots or rhizomes of the lotus plant. They have a smooth, waxy texture and crunchy, ivory-coloured flesh. When cooked, starches are released, bringing out the root's faint, natural sweetness and nutty quality. Choose roots that are firm, with smooth, unblemished skin.

18. Dried persimmons

Dried persimmons have a sweet and chewy texture and can be enjoyed on their own as a tasty snack or added to desserts.

19. Pine nuts

Pine nuts are harvested from pine cones. Store them in the refrigerator or freezer to prevent them from spoiling, especially in humid climates.

20. Radish sprouts

Radish sprouts are germinated radish seeds which have just begun to put out leaves. They have a sweet, vegetal flavour that adds crunch to salads and dishes.

22

20

23

25

21

24

26

21. Rice cakes

Made of rice flour, water and salt, these rice cakes are available from Korean supermarkets. They have a firm chewy texture and take on the flavour of the dish readily. The Chinese also have a similar variety of rice cakes which can be used if the Korean variety is not available.

22. Seaweed (*wakame*)

Wakame is a sea vegetable or edible seaweed. It has a subtly sweet flavour and is most often served in soups and salads.

23. Dried somen noodles

Somen noodles are very thin, white Japanese noodles made of wheat flour. They are sold in dried form in bundles, and are readily available from Korean or Japanese supermarkets.

24. Fermented soy bean paste

Made from fermented soy beans, Korean soy bean paste or *dwenjang* has a mild, sweet flavour. It differs in taste from most common varieties of Asian soy bean paste and should not be substituted.

25. Soy bean sprouts

Also known as *kongnamul*, soy bean sprouts feature heavily in Korean dishes. They are also a base ingredient in *dwenjang*.

26. White radish

White radish is also popularly known as daikon. They have an elongate shape, and are usually larger in diameter than the common red carrot. Radishes are readily available all year round. Choose radishes that are firm without blemishes.

weights and measures

Quantities for this book are given in Metric, Imperial and American (spoon) measures. Standard spoon and cup measurements used are: 1 tsp = 5 ml, 1 Tbsp = 15 ml, 1 cup = 250 ml. All measures are level unless otherwise stated.

LIQUID AND VOLUME MEASURES

Metric	Imperial	American
5 ml	$^1/_6$ fl oz	1 teaspoon
10 ml	$^1/_3$ fl oz	1 dessertspoon
15 ml	$^1/_2$ fl oz	1 tablespoon
60 ml	2 fl oz	$^1/_4$ cup (4 tablespoons)
85 ml	$2^1/_2$ fl oz	$^1/_3$ cup
90 ml	3 fl oz	$^3/_8$ cup (6 tablespoons)
125 ml	4 fl oz	$^1/_2$ cup
180 ml	6 fl oz	$^3/_4$ cup
250 ml	8 fl oz	1 cup
300 ml	10 fl oz ($^1/_2$ pint)	$1^1/_4$ cups
375 ml	12 fl oz	$1^1/_2$ cups
435 ml	14 fl oz	$1^3/_4$ cups
500 ml	16 fl oz	2 cups
625 ml	20 fl oz (1 pint)	$2^1/_2$ cups
750 ml	24 fl oz ($1^1/_5$ pints)	3 cups
1 litre	32 fl oz ($1^3/_5$ pints)	4 cups
1.25 litres	40 fl oz (2 pints)	5 cups
1.5 litres	48 fl oz ($2^2/_5$ pints)	6 cups
2.5 litres	80 fl oz (4 pints)	10 cups

DRY MEASURES

Metric	Imperial
30 grams	1 ounce
45 grams	$1^1/_2$ ounces
55 grams	2 ounces
70 grams	$2^1/_2$ ounces
85 grams	3 ounces
100 grams	$3^1/_2$ ounces
110 grams	4 ounces
125 grams	$4^1/_2$ ounces
140 grams	5 ounces
280 grams	10 ounces
450 grams	16 ounces (1 pound)
500 grams	1 pound, $1^1/_2$ ounces
700 grams	$1^1/_2$ pounds
800 grams	$1^3/_4$ pounds
1 kilogram	2 pounds, 3 ounces
1.5 kilograms	3 pounds, $4^1/_2$ ounces
2 kilograms	4 pounds, 6 ounces

OVEN TEMPERATURE

	°C	°F	Gas Regulo
Very slow	120	250	1
Slow	150	300	2
Moderately slow	160	325	3
Moderate	180	350	4
Moderately hot	190/200	370/400	5/6
Hot	210/220	410/440	6/7
Very hot	230	450	8
Super hot	250/290	475/550	9/10

LENGTH

Metric	Imperial
0.5 cm	$^1/_4$ inch
1 cm	$^1/_2$ inch
1.5 cm	$^3/_4$ inch
2.5 cm	1 inch

index